100 MORE ACTIVITIES
FOR PRESCHOOLERS

A big thanks to all of our contributors:
Chris Behnke
Deborah Berkimer
Karen Brigham
Nancy Brown
Robin Currie
Anna Marie Dahlquist
Carl Heine
Neta Jackson
Lois Keffer
Debbie Powell
Donald and Brenda Ratcliff
Laurie Riddle
Judy Stonecipher
Beth Swale
Anna Trimiew
Ramona Warren

100 MORE ACTIVITIES FOR PRESCHOOLERS

© 1991 by David C. Cook Publishing Co.

Cook Ministry Resources
a division of Cook Communications Ministries
4050 Lee Vance View, Colorado Springs, CO 80918-7100

Printed in the United States of America

Designed by Christopher Patchel and Elizabeth Thompson

ISBN: 1-55513-454-8

CONTENTS

Bible Story Activities
Learning Activities
Games
Character Building Activities
Bulletin Board and Mural Activities
Family Activities
Just for Fun Activities
Holiday Activities

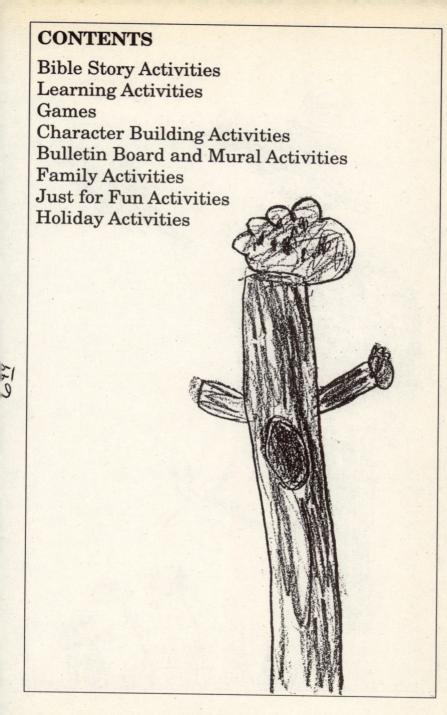

113794

BIBLE STORY ACTIVITIES

1 God Separates the Water

Demonstrate God separating the water from the land in this way. Fill a large dishpan 1/4 full of sand and add a few large rocks. Add water until sand and rocks are covered. Push the sand to one side with one hand and the "land" and "mountains" will appear.

2 God Cares for Birds

Gather around a parakeet, canary, or other pet bird in a cage. Encourage the children to talk in soft voices so as not to frighten it. If the bird is tame, bring it out on your finger; otherwise just watch it in its cage.

Help the children enjoy the bird by asking some of the following questions:

What colors are the bird's feathers?

How did the bird get dressed this morning?

What kind of sound does the bird make?

What does it eat?

3 Find the Lost Sheep

After telling the Bible story of Jesus and the lost sheep, talk about what a difficult task it was to find a little lost sheep in the night with no flashlight. Explain that the shepherd would have had to use his ears to listen carefully for the sound of the sheep. Then let children play a game of blind tag called "Find the Lost Sheep." The "lost sheep" will stand or hide somewhere in the room and say a soft "baa" every few seconds. The rest of the children must keep their eyes closed and search for the sheep using only their hands and their ears. The child who finds the sheep gets to be the "lost sheep" in the next round.

4 Hungry Lambs

In this game one child is chosen as a shepherd. The shepherd's job is to tag the hungry lambs who are "baaing." This quiets the sheep. After each hungry lamb is tagged, he or she must count to ten before "baaing" again. See if the shepherd can get everyone quiet at once.

5 Wolf!

Choose one child to be a shepherd and another to be a wolf. All the rest play sheep. During play, the wolves make the sound of "grrrr" and the sheep "baaa." Sheep try to stay away from wolves, but if tagged by a wolf, that "sheep" becomes a wolf. All wolves try to tag sheep without being tagged by the shepherd. If the shepherd tags a wolf, the wolf becomes a sheep again. Play for a minute at a time. Count to see how many sheep are left. Play several times with different starting characters. Stay within a designated area.

6 What's It Like?

This activity will be especially meaningful if done after either the story of blind Bartimaeus or the ten lepers. Preschoolers may never have thought about what it feels like to miss out on things because of a physical disability. This activity will give children the opportunity to find out what it's like to be blind, or to be without the use of a leg.

Let volunteers take turns being blindfolded. Have each volunteer feel the face of two or three children and try to guess who they are. Use the blindfold to tie a volunteer's leg in a bent position. Have the volunteers try to walk, pushing a small chair in front of them for balance. Talk about how Jesus showed His love for people with special needs by taking time to notice their problems and heal them.

7 Fishing for Good News

Cover a large box with a blue sheet or blanket. Children cast string with a bent paper clip hook into the "water." Sit behind the box, attaching a paper fish to the lines thrown in. On the fish should be written a Bible verse.

8 Tea Party

After telling the story of Jesus at the home of Simon the Pharisee, let children give a "tea party" of their own. Food can be "pretend," or you might choose to have lemonade and graham crackers for the children to serve. Choose one child to be the host, one to be the honored guest, and have the rest take the parts of the other guests. Let children dress up in old adult clothing from a dress-up trunk. Encourage everyone to be very polite and friendly at their tea party!

9 Riding the Donkey

Children line up as for "London Bridge." They pass through the "gate to Jerusalem" as they sing these words to the tune.

Riding to Jerusalem
Through the gate, through the gate.
Riding to Jerusalem
On a donkey!

When children are "caught," give each one a palm branch to wave as the game continues.

LEARNING ACTIVITIES

10 My Own Garden

Give each child a piece of brown paper or section of brown paper bag. On it, they may paste pictures cut from catalogs or magazines of things they would like to grow in a garden. Remind children that God made all the plants and He wants us to take care of them.

11 Alive and Not Alive

With masking tape, make two large circles on the floor. Label one circle "Alive" and the second "Not Alive." Collect items that are alive (plants, small animals, and pictures of people) and not alive (chairs, toy trucks, and rocks). Talk to the children about living things—they breathe, grow, need food and oxygen. Talk about nonliving things and compare them to living things. Put each item you have collected in the appropriate circle on the floor. Remove the items from the circles and let children categorize them. Remind children that God gives us life. He makes things grow.

12 Feel, Touch, and Smell

For "feel" bring an electric box fan. Turn it on and let the children feel the air blowing on them. Emphasize that we know the air is blowing even though we cannot see it.

For "touch" put several objects (such as a small rock, a crayon, a spoon, and a glove) in a small cloth bag. Have children feel the object in the bag and guess what it is. Emphasize that we know the object is there even though we do not see it.

For "smell" use foods, flowers, and other aromatic substances. Have one or two children blindfolded and guess what the objects are simply by smelling them. Let children take turns using the blindfolds. Emphasize that the objects are there even though we don't see them.

13 Traffic Signs

Show the children pictures of flash cards of different traffic signs. Have the children try to guess what the signs tell people to do. Discuss what the signs mean. Point out that road signs are rules that tell us what to do to be safe.

14 Banking Fun

Children think it's great fun to handle money, because it's usually "off-limits" to them. Bring in several old purses, wallets, and play money. If you have a box of coins, let the children play with those. Or, let them look at a collection of foreign money. Talk about the similarities and differences of the money of different countries.

Let the children play bank, and decide what part of their money they will save, what they will spend, and what they will give to help others. Explain at the beginning of the activity that you're not really giving them money—it's just for play, and you will collect it all at the end. Praise God for giving us the money we need to live, plus enough to share with others.

15 Little Seeds Grow

Provide moistened potting soil and disposable planting containers such as margarine tubs. Let the children spoon soil into the planters and push seeds down in the dirt. Beans sprout well and quickly. Sunflowers are also successful and when transplanted grow taller than the children. Growing plants is a very special way of experiencing God's miracles of growth.

16 Feed the Birds

Give each child a piece of bread. Help them to remove the crusts and set aside. Show the children how to mold the bread into a ball. Help the children tie a length of string or yarn around the ball of bread. Take the bread outside and tie onto a low tree or bush branches. Scatter the bread crusts on the ground. Tell children that the birds will also use the string or yarn in building nests.

17 Being the Teacher

Most children really enjoy an opportunity to take center stage. Allow them to take turns being the teacher. Talk about how Jesus went around teaching people, and that teaching about God's love is very important work. Give children a choice about what to teach. It may be a Bible verse, a mini sermon or a song. A few articles of old adult clothing will add to the fun of the activity.

18 Footprints

As you visit the zoo, take along some paper to sketch on. Look for as many different kinds of animal footprints as you can find. Draw a simple copy of each and let your child help to label them. Talk about how God created animals with certain kinds of feet to do special things, like the duck's webbed ones which help in swimming.

19 Who Are You?

Have the children sit in a circle. Talk briefly with them about our identity with families. Ask the question, "Who are you?" The children will answer by giving their name. You may want to go around the circle several times. Each time have the children answer a different way (by gender, "I'm a girl," or by age, "I'm four years old.")

20 Everything God Made Was Good

Staple three sheets of white paper between two sheets of construction paper. On the front write "Everything God Made Was Good." Inside, the children may paste pictures cut from magazines of different things God made. How wonderful to have a book of God's creation to read over and over again.

21 Surprise Bag of Teaching Things

Fill a paper bag with items such as a mixing spoon, story book, crayon, ball, and Bible. As items are pulled from the bag, have children identify them and how they are used by adults to teach children things.

22 Who Goes to Church?

Glue pictures of people and objects around the edges of several paper plates. Children can attach clothespins to the pictures of people that can worship God in church.

23 All Kinds of Houses

Give each child an 8 1/2" x 11" paper and a choice of various paper shapes including big and small squares, triangles, and rectangles. Let them each construct a house by laying out the shapes and pasting them down.

24 Taking Care of Others

While looking at books and pictures, help children suggest ways they can help care for plants and animals. What are some things they can do when they're older? Can they start now caring for things in a small way?

25 Love Chain

This activity will give children a graphic representation of the people in the church who love them. Give each child a strip of paper 4" x 1/2". Help them think of someone in the church who loves them. Write the name of that person on the paper strip of the first child and form into a ring. Continue in this manner, interlocking rings to form a chain. Children can keep adding links as long as there are people to name. A pictorial directory will be helpful. How long is the love chain for your class?

26 Our Families

Put out clay or play dough. As children cut out cookie-cutter people, arrange them in family groups representing the children's families. This will help you get to know the families of each child and give the children another opportunity to thank God for their families.

27 Protection Inspection

In this activity children will make an "inspection glass" (to look like a magnifying glass) by gluing two 4" construction paper circles with the centers cut out to a craft stick. You might want to glue clear kitchen wrap in the "glass" to make it look authentic. Children can use these to look for signs that parents and adults care for them, or to see signs of God's work in our world.

28 I'm Looking for a Friend

Give one child a beanbag. That child walks around the circle while you sing these words to the tune *Farmer in the Dell*.

I'm looking for a friend.
I'm looking for a friend.
Drop the beanbag, 1, 2, 3.
I'm looking for a friend.

The child drops the beanbag behind a friend and takes that child's place in the circle so there is a new person walking with the beanbag.

29 Night and Day

Have the children sit in a circle. Show two pieces of paper, one white and one black. Explain that white makes us think of day, which is light, while black makes us think of night which is dark. Place both sheets in the middle of the circle.

Your children can take turns tossing a beanbag. If it lands on black, they state something about the night; if it lands on white, they say something about day.

30 Whatever Is It?

Draw things in the air with your finger and have children guess what they are. You may need to give the children clues. Here are some examples:

Draw a large, round sun with sunbeams.
Clue: **It shines in the sky and keeps us warm.**
Draw a tree.
Clue: **It has leaves and fruit grows on it sometimes.**

31 Name Game

Ask the children to sit in a circle. Have the first child say his or her name. Have the second child repeat the first child's name and say his or her own name and so on around the circle. You or your helper should be the last one to say all the names. And you or your helper might need to help the children in repeating the names of the others.

32 Who Is My Friend?

Have the children sit in a circle. The leader should start the game by asking, "Can you guess who my friend is?" One clue should be given such as, "My friend is wearing a green dress." Continue giving clues until the children have guessed who the person is (be sure the friend you are describing is in the circle). The child that guessed the identity of the friend should take a turn or go around the circle giving each child a turn to describe someone else.

33 A Friend Loves

Have children sit in a circle on the floor. The leader should walk around the circle, tapping each child on the head while repeating, "A friend loves at all times." After a few taps say, "A friend loves when . . ." The child whose head is tapped this last time should offer an example of when a friend loves (e.g., when a friend shares a toy, when a child prays for a friend, when a child lets a friend go first at the water fountain). This child should then be the "leader." Be sure each child gets a turn to be "leader."

34 Mother/Father Says

Play a variation of "Simon Says" using the words "Mother (or Father) says . . ." If the instruction is, "Sweep the floor," children should stay still. If the instruction is, "Mother (or Father) says sweep the floor," children should do the action. Children must listen closely.

35 Join the Circle

In this activity, the leader will choose children from the group, two at a time, to join in a circle. Each time the leader chooses new children, the leader will say, "God loves Cindy" or "God loves Matthew," using the name of each child. Then they will all join hands and walk in a circle while singing the following song to the tune of *God Is So Good*.

God loves us all.
God loves us all.
God loves us all.
He loves you and me!

Keep adding children, two at a time, and singing the song each time until the whole group is holding hands and walking in a circle.

36 Good Teachers

Play a game of "musical chairs" where everyone is a winner. Set chairs in a row with enough chairs for everyone to be seated. Play music on the cassette tape recorder or record player. When the music stops children are seated, and you may choose one child to name someone who can tell him or her about Jesus. Give the children who name someone (even with help) a sticker of Jesus to wear.

37 Name the Helper

In this game, children will act out various types of jobs that helpers do. (Pretending to preach like a pastor, to spray a building like a fire fighter, etc.) The rest of the class tries to guess the helper being acted out. The children may choose a helper or take a suggestion from the leader.

38 Guess Who?

Divide children into two groups. Hold up a sheet between them. Group one will be guessers, group two will choose one person at a time to stick his or her foot under the sheet so the guessers can see it. Can the guessers guess who? Give each child in group two a turn to stick a foot under the sheet and be guessed, then switch sides.

39 Obey the Rules

To play this game you will need a piece of red paper and a piece of green paper. Children stand behind a line and the leader says, "Rules are important to obey. When I hold up the green paper, all children may take a step forward. When I hold up the red, all children stand still." Since the children are moving at the same speed they should all cross the finish line at the same time and be winners.

40 Who Am I?

Whisper the name of a bird, animal, or plant to a child. The child can say, "Who Am I?" then act out his or her bird, animal, or plant. Other children can guess.

If a child has trouble knowing what to do, here are a few suggestions:

Bird—pecking out of a shell, flapping wings, or pecking seeds from ground.

Flower—crouch down, then slowly stand up with hands together overhead; open hands to represent flower.

Squirrel—hold nut in hands and nibble; scurry around.

41 Musical Disciples

One child stands in the center of the circle with eyes closed. Children march around the circle until the music stops. Child in the center raises arm and points to one child who gets to be the next one in the circle. Remind children that no one gets to be chosen all the time, but each of them is special to Jesus.

42 Divided Picture of Kind Deeds

Find five or six pictures of people doing kind things. Magazines and old Sunday school papers are good sources for this. Mount pictures on different-colored construction paper, then cut mounted pictures in half. Hide the divided pictures around the room and hunt for them. Match the pieces and name the helper.

43 How Do I Know?

This guessing game is played by describing something and asking children to guess what you're describing. For example, you might say, "I am thinking of something that's juicy, sweet, red, round, and good to eat. What is it?" (The answer is apple.) When someone guesses the right answer, allow them to whisper to you, the next item to be described.

44 Toss and Grow

Use a baby blanket and a soft ball. Children can hold corners and edges of the blanket. One child tosses the ball into the center of the blanket and all pull on the blanket to make it bounce. As you do this they can say "Thank You, God, that (child's name) is growing up." When the ball bounces off the blanket, another child may toss it in and be the subject of the refrain.

45 Let's Visit a Friend

Children can play a simple game about going to see a friend. As you go around the circle, each one says, "When I go to see my friend, I like to take_____" (insert something friends would enjoy together). If children really like this game, they could go around again, and add something new to take on their visit, saying both things the second time around.

46 God Is with Me

The leader has cards with pictures of various places on them such as a doctor's office, school building, house, etc. Holding cards down so she/he can't see the pictures, the leader invites a child to draw one card. All of the children can see the card, but not the leader. The leader then has to guess which picture is on the card. When the correct guess is made the leader says, "God is with us when we're at (name the place pictured on the card)."

CHARACTER-BUILDING ACTIVITIES

47 Building a Prayer Place

Provide very large blocks or cardboard boxes and let the children build an enclosure several levels high. Describe it as a special place to pray. Encourage them to pray a short prayer in their enclosure. Also stress that Jesus is with us wherever we are, but sometimes people like to have special places to pray. Ask them if there is a special place at their house where they would like to pray.

48 Helping Pennies

Trace around pennies on a large chart. When children bring pennies they can tape them to the chart. When the chart is filled the class can use the money to help others.

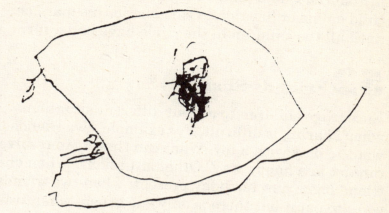

49 Frosting Cookies

Provide the children with sugar cookies or graham crackers to spread with canned icing. Let them each make two treats, one to eat and one to share.

50 Going to Church

Use dress-up clothes such as aprons, ties, belts, and coats to portray adults. (Avoid shoes and hats for health reasons.) Dress baby dolls and take them to church. The children will thank God for adults who take them to church.

51 My Friends

Children should sit in a circle. The children can practice introducing each other. The leader should start by saying "Hi, my name is [insert name] and this is my friend [child on the right]." The child introduced would then do the same—introducing the child on his or her right. Continue in this manner until all the children in the circle have had a turn.

52 Friends Share

Encourage children to act out different situations when sharing is difficult. For example, two friends want to play with a toy. What can they do to resolve conflict in a happy way? Other situations: When one friend has a new birthday present; when two friends want to paint but there is only one brush; when two friends are playing a game and a third child comes along. Talk about how they feel when they share and how they feel when they don't share.

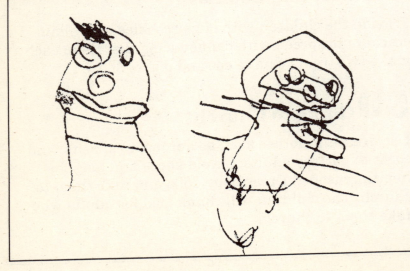

53 I Want to Share

Children should sit on the floor in a circle, legs extended and feet touching the foot of the person on the right and the left. The leader says, "I want to share this ball with (child's name)," and roll the ball to that child. That child then chooses another friend and says, "I want to share this ball with (second child's name)," and rolls the ball. The leader may suggest names so that every child gets one or more turns to share.

Alternative: Children may sit on chairs. The leader holds a toy enjoyed by both girls and boys (ball, stuffed animal, etc.) and says, "I want to share this toy with (child's name)," then gets up and walks over to chosen child and gives the toy. That child then chooses another child to receive the toy, and so on.

54 Hide-a-Treat

This fun activity will help children see the importance of sharing. Before the session begins, hide several wrapped candies around the room. Make sure there is one piece per child. At an appropriate time in your discussion about sharing, tell the children that you have brought a treat to share with all of them, but they're going to have to find it. Give instructions that no one should eat the treat, just find one and sit back down.

Discuss with the children that you shared a treat with them and they shared, too, by finding just one candy so that everyone could enjoy a treat.

55 Wash 'n Scrub

Children like to play at cleaning up, and it's an important part of the way they learn. Things like squirt bottles, paper towels, and dishpans full of suds are a fascinating invitation to fun. So let them go at it!

You may wish to make simple cleaning smocks from large paper grocery bags to protect clothes from splashes. Cut a seam up the back, and nice, big comfortable holes for neck and arms. You will need a large garbage bag to hold the used paper towels and "smocks." Be sure to praise the children for the excellent job they did!

56 Chenille Wire People

Bend the middle of a long chenille wire into a small round loop for the head. Straighten the two ends and use them as legs. Wrap a shorter wire around the middle of the figure for arms. Use these figures for acting out family situations, ways of praise and worship, or ways of apologizing with hugs or prayers.

57 People of God

Give each child a paper plate. After they draw pictures of their faces on them, add yarn hair. On mural paper, draw stick figures and attach the paper plate heads. God loves all of them!

58 God Loves You!

After you have experienced God's love together, share it! Children can trace and cut out red paper hearts. On each write, "God loves you!" Give each child two or three to give to family and friends during the week. If there are extras, mail some to a shut-in or any children absent from this activity.

59 Kind Friends

Give each child a partner. Let them explore the room or outside looking for pennies or hidden notes. The notes can have a Bible verse on it about friends.

60 Helpers

Preschoolers sometimes feel they can't help because painting the house or mowing the lawn are jobs that are too big. Comment on instances you see of children helping others such as picking up crayons, throwing away papers, or handing out drinks. Tell children you are grateful to God that they can be such good helpers. Have children suggest other ways they can be helpers in the classroom.

61 Church Friends

Building a church with blocks will require coopera-
tion and help. After the church is built, each child
can make a figure from chenille wires to represent
someone going to church. You may wish to have
them make pews and other church furniture out of
small boxes. The children can use the church they
built to worship God for friends.

62 Babies Welcome

Let the children set up a nursery. Use shoe boxes for
beds with scrap material for blankets. Child-sized
chairs and cloth scraps for diapers plus assorted
feeding utensils will provide a place to talk about
family care and love.

MURAL AND BULLETIN BOARDS

63 Who Does Jesus Love?

On mural paper, write the words "Who does Jesus love?" Provide children with people pictures cut from magazines and catalogs. If possible you may use an instant camera to add the children's pictures to the mural, too. After the picture is complete, answer the question: Everyone!

64 Reasons for Seasons

Divide a paper into four sections. In each, draw a simple frame house. Children will add various objects to show different seasons. You might try cotton balls for snow or clouds, strips of tin foil for rain, torn green tissue paper for grass, and stickers of birds and flowers. God made each season so plants and animals can live and grow.

65 Healthful Foods Collage

Provide a large sheet of butcher paper and an assortment of old magazines for the children. Let them choose pictures of nutritious foods from magazines. Help them paste these to butcher paper. Talk about how Jesus wants us to be healthy and that includes being smart about what we eat.

66 Class Rules Mural

Most children don't mind a few rules, especially if they have some say in setting them! Let your children help establish a few rules for your worship time. Discuss what's most important to keep your time together fun and enjoyable for everyone. Explain that the rules need to be clear and simple, and that you don't want too many. Let children make suggestions as you jot them down. Write your final list of three to five rules on a long sheet of shelf paper. Let the children draw pictures to illustrate each rule.

67 Who Can Help?

Divide mural paper into sections for each child. Children can paste pictures in their section that show people helping others. At the top write "Who can help?" Label each section with the name of the child who added the pictures.

68 God Loves Us All!

Trace the hands and feet of each child onto colored paper. Cut them out and paste on mural paper with the name of each child by the appropriate cut outs. Isn't it wonderful that even though we are all different we can work together to make something as special as this mural?

69 Praise Him

Let children choose from magazine and catalog pictures things they would like to paste onto a mural. Title the display, "Reasons to Thank Jesus." It is important that even preschoolers realize the source of all good things is Jesus and His love.

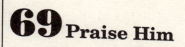

FAMILY ACTIVITIES

70 Prayer Sticks

Glue pictures of individual family members and friends to craft sticks. Store them in an envelope or small jar. At family prayer time, have your child pull out a stick and pray for the person whose picture is on it.

71 God Made Colors

Help your child appreciate all of the colors God made by having special color days around the house. For example, on "Red Day" help your child dress in red clothes. Serve something red at each meal (strawberry jam, spaghetti, or apples). If you have time to go for a walk, try to find all the red things you can.

72 Building a Prayer

Help your child build a prayer by asking what he or she wants to pray about. You can suggest the child include different kinds of things: things to be thankful for, things to ask God for, expressions of praise or love for God, etc. To begin the prayer, mention a thanksgiving and have the child pray a sentence prayer; mention a request and have the child pray another simple sentence, etc.

73 Clean As All Outdoors

Go outside and do activities that show care for the environment. Picking up garbage, raking leaves, sweeping steps can all be done with child-sized tools. Children can even weed the garden with some direction.

74 Prayer Chain

Make a group or family prayer chain. Use strips of construction paper about 1" x 8". Use one color for prayer requests, another for thanksgivings, and a third for answered prayers. Form each strip into a circle and tape or staple the ends together after slipping it through the last "chain." Add a few each day.

JUST FOR FUN ACTIVITIES

75 Picture Pose

Look at picture books of families helping one another. Encourage the children to "picture pose" some of the pictures. That means they get into the same positions as the people in the picture. They can also act out what they think happens next.

76 Finger Flowers

Provide circle stickers and several ink pads. Place a sticker on paper for the center of the flower. Children press their fingers onto the pad and then onto the paper around the sticker to form the petals of the flower. Children will praise God for the wonders of spring.

77 Nature Squish Bags

To let children handle some of the things God made put sand, loose dirt, or water in freezer bags that snap closed. (You may want to double bag the items and seal them with masking tape to avoid spills.) Then have children put their hands behind their backs and instruct them not to look at the bags you will give them. See if they can figure out what's in the bag without looking.

78 Bubble Prints

Make bubble print cards by mixing 1/4 cup water, 20 drops of liquid food coloring, and 2 tablespoons of liquid detergent in a large bowl. Make a mound of bubbles using an eggbeater. Then lay a piece of paper over the bubbles, causing them to adhere to the paper. Paper will soon be covered with the prints of popped bubbles. Use the paper to make cards.

79 Family Puppets

Give each child a craft stick to represent each member of the family. Children can add features with markers, then glue on scraps of material for clothing and yarn for hair.

80 Building a Wall

Use shoe boxes to make building blocks that don't make much noise. Tape the boxes shut. Children can stack them to make buildings.

81 Musical Instruments

Children can make the following simple instruments:

Kazoo—Fold wax paper over the teeth of a pocket comb. Hold in place with rubber bands on each end. Hum on the comb to make kazoo sounds.

Bells—String several small bells on a piece of ribbon or string about 6" long. Tie and shake.

82 Messy Friends

Children will each choose a partner. Each pair will work on one picture with finger paint. This may be messy so make sure the area and children's clothing are protected. Painting with a friend is twice the fun!

83 More Than Blocks

Some small toys added to the block area will expand imaginations and make learning fun. Include small figures of people, cars and other transportation, and street signs cut from paper and taped to a craft stick in a mound of clay. Use the additional figures to talk about obeying, sharing, and cooperating.

84 Going on a Picnic

No matter how miserable the weather is outside, you can pretend to go on a picnic. Think of what you would pack and then carry the picnic basket and blanket around the room until you find a good place. Give thanks before serving a small snack.

85 Signs to Obey

Help children glue red, yellow, and green circles on a rectangle of black paper to make a traffic signal. Then teach them to point to the colors as you say this rhyme.

**Stop and sing a song of joy.
Wait for your friends and share your toys.
Go tell everyone you know
Our Lord Jesus loves you so!**

86 Quiet Pets

Collect smooth stones for the bodies of animals. Glue on paper legs, a head, and a tail or form these features from chenille wires. Add wiggle eyes and use tempera paint to add markings. How many different animals are there in your zoo? God made them all!

87 Telephone

Tie loops in the ends of a piece of string. Place the loops over the thumbs of two children. They can pretend to talk to each other by holding up the thumb for an earpiece and little finger for a mouthpiece. Make the string short enough that it does not tangle around others. What good news can they share on the phone?

88 Find a Friend's Name

In advance, print a pair of children's names on two slips of paper. Hide the slips of paper in fairly obvious places in the room. Tell the children to search for the slip with their own name, pick it up, and sit down to wait until everyone has found their name. Help children "read" their friend's name on the slips of paper. Let the pairs of friends go to an activity center together.

89 Rub-a-Dub-Dub

Explore the texture of different items by doing "rubbings." Place a sheet of paper over the item and rub over the area with a crayon or soft pencil. Notice the patterns that appear!

Nature rubbings: Use flat items, such as leaves, pressed flowers, and tree bark.

Building materials: Do rubbings of brick, wood, and cement.

Household items: Try book covers with embossed or raised print, a cheese grater, and a lace doily.

90 Spring Walk

On a paper, draw simple line drawings of spring things such as flowers, birds, and leaves. Talk about these things with the children. Then take a walk around the church. Have children watch for the spring things on your list and check them off. This will focus the children's attention and encourage them to observe God's wonderful world more closely.

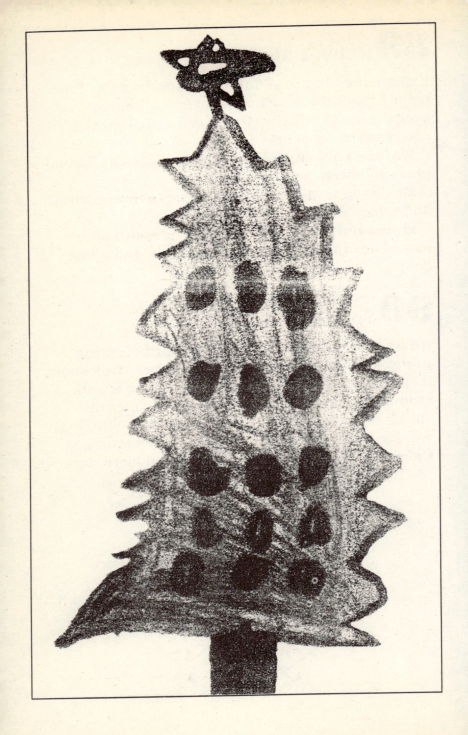

HOLIDAY ACTIVITIES

91 Cookie Wreaths

Christmas is a wonderful time to reinforce the idea of sharing with others. Remind the children that God shared His very dearest and precious treasure with us—His Son, Jesus! As a fun activity, choose your favorite round, store-bought cookies (butter cookies work well) and let children decorate them with tube-type cake-decorating icing. Have children share them with another class.

92 Prayer Bells

For a Christmas activity that emphasizes our need to help each other by praying, supply children with 5" bell-shaped patterns and construction paper. After children have traced and cut them out, glue a picture of a missionary, friend, or family member on one side. Attach yarn to the bell and hang on the Christmas tree. At family prayer time, you may want to let your child choose one person to pray for.

93 Pass the News

This is a version of the old "telephone" game. The players sit in a circle. The first person whispers something into the ear of the person to his or her right such as "Praise God." That person then passes the news onto the person to his or her right and so on. When the message comes back to the last person, he or she says it out loud. The only kind of message the players may pass is good news. (Tip: When playing at Christmastime, the children may be asked to think of Christmas good news such as "God sent Jesus," "Jesus is born," or "It happened in Bethlehem.")

94 Wrapping Baby Jesus in Swaddling Clothes

Traditional renditions of the Christmas story—especially those based on the King James Version of the Bible—may tell of Jesus being wrapped in "swaddling clothes" after He was born (Luke 2:7, 12). Modern-day children may be mystified by this reference. Explain that swaddling clothes were like a modern-day baby blanket. In biblical times they were narrow strips of cloth in which a newborn baby was wrapped for warmth and comfort. Provide a doll, a cradle, and strips of soft, white cloth, and let each child take a turn pretending to wrap Baby Jesus in "swaddling clothes," love Him, and then put Him in the "manger." (If possible, embellish the cradle with straw to make it more like a manger.)

95 Hide the Ornament

Show an unbreakable Christmas ornament. While everyone closes their eyes, hide the ornament; then tell the children to look for it silently. When they "find" it, they should not point to it or say anything, but just come sit down. When the last person discovers the ornament and sits down, ask the first child who "found" it to show where it was hidden.

96 Love Gifts for Jesus

Help children think about ways they can "give gifts of love to Jesus" at Christmastime. Remind them that when we do kind things for others, we are showing love for Jesus.

Older preschoolers can help think of ideas, such as: Help clear the supper table; hug someone who needs cheering up; give pennies to church; help pick up toys cheerfully; don't hit back; etc. Write each idea on a slip of paper and put it in a box with wrapping paper on it. (For younger preschoolers, write the ideas ahead of time and put them in the box.) Let each child draw out one slip of paper. Read what it says. Encourage each child to do what the paper says this week as a gift of love to Jesus.

97 Egg Hunt

Hide paper eggs around the room for the children to find. When they bring an egg to you put a sticker of Jesus on it. Finding eggs is one happy thing to do in spring, but the happiest thing of all is to rejoice because Jesus is alive.

98 Thank You, God, for . . .

Thanksgiving comes only once a year, but every day we have things for which to be thankful. Children can paste pictures cut from magazines onto heavy paper and make stick figures from the items by attaching to craft sticks. Wave the sticks as you sing these words to the tune *Farmer in the Dell*.

We give thanks to God.
We give thanks to God.
God made all things that are good.
Thank You, thank You, God.

99 Thank You, God, for Family and Friends

Cut out a string of paper dolls in advance for each child. Have them glue the dolls on a sheet of construction paper. Then let children dress the dolls using fabric scraps, markers, and crayons. As they work on their projects, talk with them about some of the friends God has given them. Remind them to thank God for their friends.

100 What's in the Box?

In a box, place classroom items that help your students learn about Jesus. (Teaching-aid figures, books, records or tapes, unbreakable Nativity figures, Christmas cards, and unbreakable ornaments with religious symbols.)

Have your preschoolers close their eyes, reach for an item in the bag, and try to guess what the item is.